JOY

by

Carole MacKenthun, R.S.M.
and Paulinus Dwyer, O.P.

illustrated by Vanessa Filkins

Cover by Vanessa Filkins

Songs by Frances Mann Benson and
Helen Kitchell Evans

ISBN No. 0-86653-360-5

Standardized Subject Code TA ac

Printing No. 98

Shining Star Publications
A Division of Good Apple, Inc.
Box 299
Carthage, IL 62321-0299

Unless otherwise indicated, the King James version of the Bible was used in preparing the activities in this book.

DEDICATION

To Dad
Love,
Carole

INTRODUCTION

"These things have I spoken unto you, that my joy might remain in you, and that your joy might be full." John 15:11

Jesus constantly gave joy to His people. He fed them if they were hungry, healed them if they were sick and cheered them if they were sad. He turned their "straw into gold" by sprinkling sunshine into their lonely hearts as He spoke of the Father's kingdom. The Holy Spirit gave this joy to Jesus, and Jesus gives His Spirit to all His friends so that we, too, may share the joy that He has. A sign that we are friends of Jesus is the joy in our hearts. This true joy is knowing that His spirit is within us and allowing Him to be manifested through us in our love for one another.

The purpose of this book is to aid educators in teaching children about this vibrant Fruit of the Spirit. These activities will motivate children to learn about the joy in knowing and following Jesus, sharing joy with others and receiving joy in their lives. These unique activities can be completed either individually or in a group. A Scriptural passage on joy is listed at the top of each idea, and more references are given in the back of the book for reflection or to embellish the activities.

TABLE OF CONTENTS

JOY IN FOLLOWING JESUS

HAPPINESS ROAD

"I have no greater joy than to hear that my children walk in truth." III John 4

A person is happy and feels joy when she follows God's law. Use a die and marker. Roll the die and move the correct number of spaces. If you can identify the Commandment or teaching of Jesus exemplified when your marker falls on a message, add the number shown in that square to your score. When all players have completed the course, the one with the highest total wins.

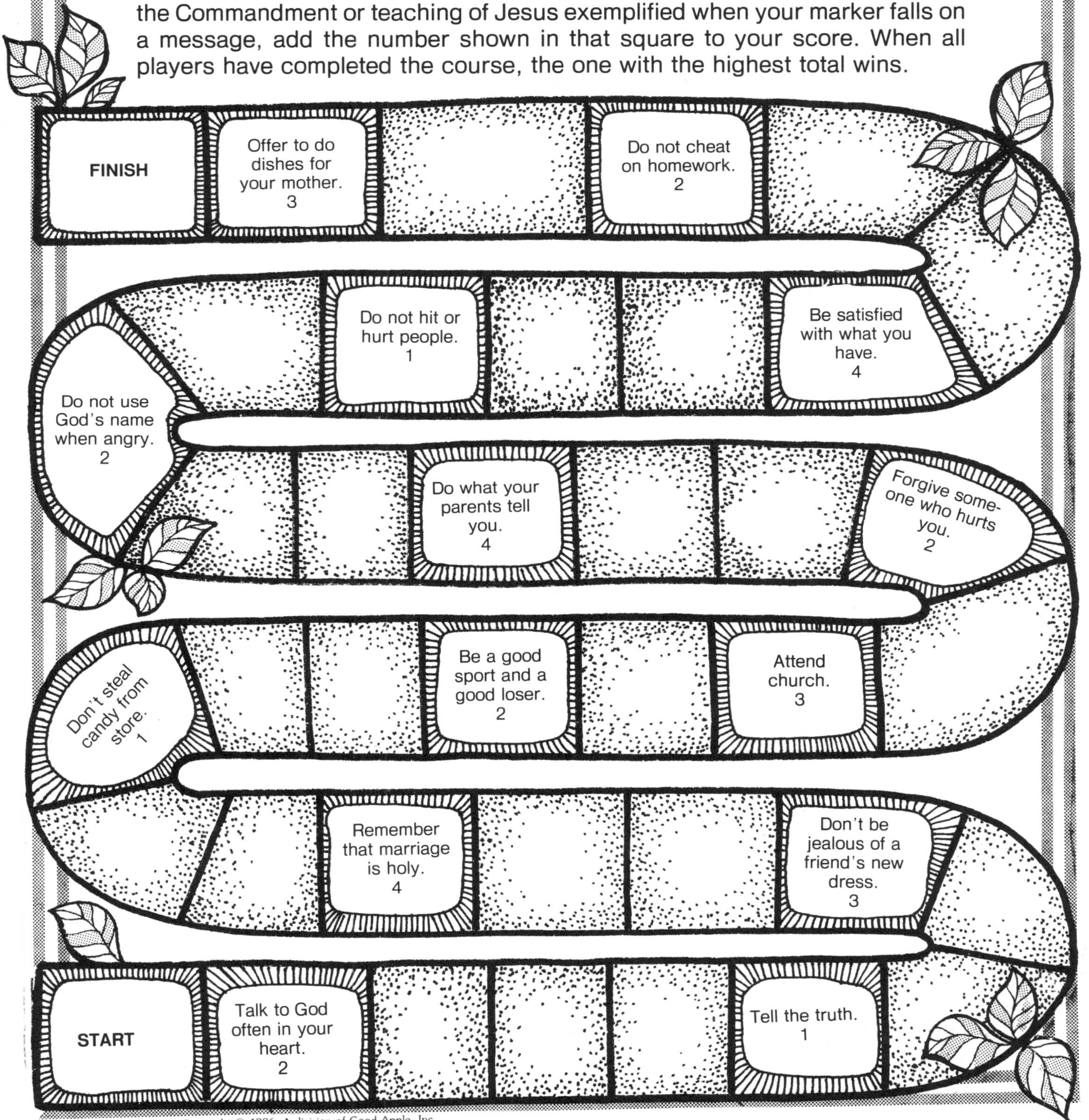

WHEEL OF HAPPINESS

"Rejoice, and be exceedingly glad; for great is your reward in heaven . . . ."
Matthew 5:12

Once Jesus went up on a mountain and taught His disciples the beatitudes. These simple statements show us how to be happy and live in the kingdom of God. The word *beatitude* means happiness. The beatitudes offer us a challenge to begin to live happily with God and His people.

Read Matthew 5:3-10 and complete the wheel below. Then attach the spinner to the center of the wheel with a brad. Use this wheel as a guide for remembering the beatitudes.

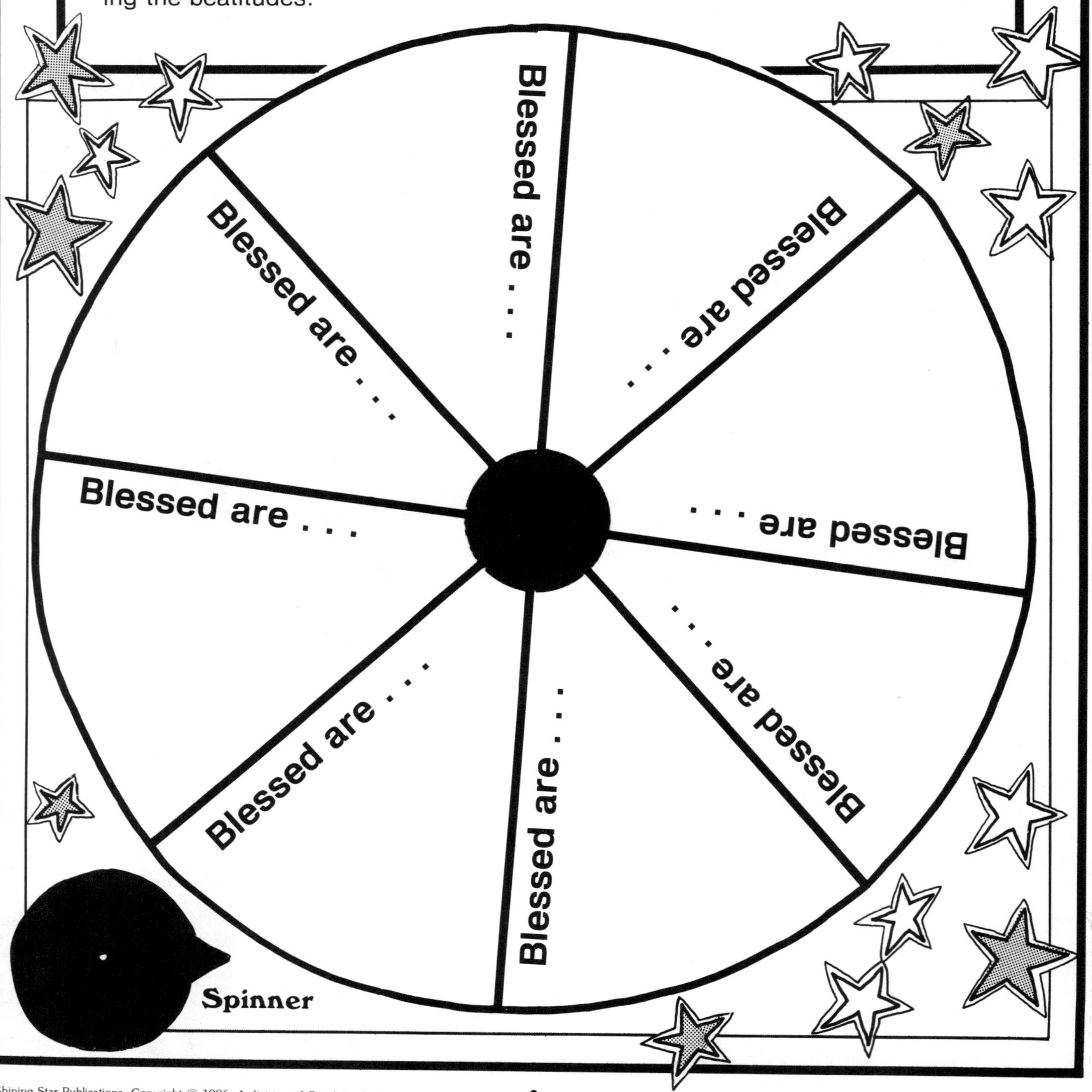

HELPS FOUND

" . . . abide in my love . . . that your joy might be full." John 15:10, 11

The human problems listed below diminish joy in our lives. The biblical references are stories which Jesus gave to help us cope with these problems. Study the references, and in each of the spaces below give an example of one of these problems found in someone's life. Then explain how the person could deal with the problem.

PROBLEMS: pride, greed, anger, laziness, fear, unwillingness to forgive, ambition, hatred

BIBLE REFERENCES: Matthew 7:1-5; Luke 6:27-31; Luke 15:25-32; Mark 11:25,26; Luke 6:37,38; Matthew 18:15; Luke 12:13-21; Mark 4:16-20; Matthew 6:25; Matthew 18:1-4; Matthew 25:1-13

*Matthew 7:1-5 (unwillingness to forgive)	*Matthew 6:25-27 (fear)
*Mark 4:16-20 fear/greed/ pride	Mark 10:20-22 or LUKE 12:13-21 (greed)
*Matthew 18:1-4 ambition	*Luke 6:27-31 hatred/forgiveness

ROAD BLOCKS

"If ye keep my commandments, ye shall abide in my love . . . that my joy might remain in you, and that your joy might be full." John 15:10, 11

Jesus promised us joy if we keep His Commandments. Listed below are human problems that interfere with our keeping these Commandments. Jesus showed us how to cope with these problems in His parables.

Look up the references listed below and match the parable which best answers the problems.

PROBLEM	REFERENCE	PARABLE
Pride	Luke 18:9-14	
Greed	Mark 10:20-22	
Anger	Matthew 5:10	
Envy	Luke 15:25-32	
Laziness	Matthew 25:1-13.	
Fear	Matthew 6:25-27	
Unwillingness to forgive	Matthew 18:21,22	
Ambition	Luke 14:7-11	
Hatred	Matthew 5:43-48	

REFERENCES: Luke 18:9-14; Matthew 5:43-48; Luke 15:25-32; Matthew 18:21,22; Luke 12:4-7; Mark 10:20-22; Matthew 5:21; Matthew 25:1-13; Luke 14:7-11

MAZE

"Thou hast made known to me the ways of life; thou shalt make me full of joy with thy countenance." Acts 2:28

Our greatest joy will be heaven. Christ told us many things we can do to reach this place of happiness. Read His suggestions in Matthew 5:1-12. Then, as you work your way through this maze, think of ways in your life these hints can help you on your way to the happiness and joy of heaven.

JOY TRAIL

"Fulfil ye my joy . . . ." Philippians 2:2

FOLLOW THE TRAIL TO HAPPINESS

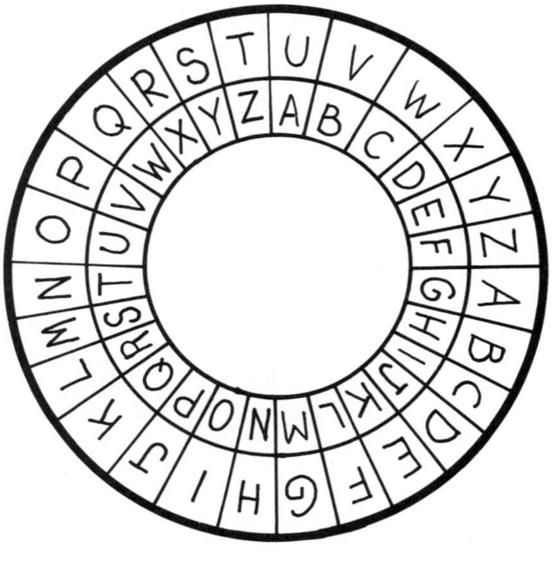

CODE WHEEL: Each letter on the outside circle stands for the letter below it on the inner circle.

DIRECTIONS:

Use the wheel to decode the message found on the trail. It is the message that God gives to help us make decisions which lead us on our way to the joy of eternal life.
Message: ______________________

____

After decoding the message, look up the entire reference cited on the trail.

Use the wheel to put the following message into code:

" . . . let them also that love thy name be joyful in thee." Psalm 5:11

RIDDLES

" . . . let me have joy of thee in the Lord . . . ."
Philemon 1:20

These are some of the people and things which shared in the most joyous event that ever happened, the resurrection of Jesus. This act gave us a promise of our greatest joy, happiness in heaven forever. See if you can solve each riddle below. Write the name of the person or thing described, and draw a picture of each.

1

We were walking very early Sunday morning. We had burial spices and were talking about how heavy the stone would be to move. Who are we?

____

2

When I came, I found the tomb empty. I thought I saw a gardener and I asked him where he had put the body. Then He called my name and I knew it was Jesus. Who am I?

____

3

I promised to come back after three days, but my disciples did not understand what I meant. I met them in many places after I arose. Who am I?

____

4

I am very heavy. I blocked the way to Jesus' tomb. Angels pushed me out of the way. What am I?

____

5

I rolled back the stone from the grave. Then I told Jesus' friends that He had risen. Who am I?

____

6

We were guarding a tomb in the caves near Calvary. Suddenly an angel came and pushed away the stone at the door of the tomb. We pretended we had been asleep when it happened. Who are we?

____

MORE RIDDLES

Here are more riddles which tell about the joy of Easter. See if you can identify them and draw pictures of each.

7

We were on our way to Emmaus when we met a man who explained all the exciting happenings in Jerusalem. We invited Him to have dinner with us and then discovered that the man was Jesus. Who are we?

____

8

Peter and I ran to the tomb. I went in after Peter and then saw that the cloths were lying there, but Jesus was gone. Who am I?

____

9

We had this imposter put to death. Then the soldiers came and told us about the empty tomb. We paid them to say that someone stole the body when they were asleep. Who are we?

____

10

They told me that Jesus had risen. I would not believe it unless I could actually put my fingers into the place where the nails had been. Who am I?

____

11

We had been wrapped around the body of Jesus. One of us was lying separate from the others. What are we?

____

12

John and I ran to the tomb when the women told us that Jesus had risen. John waited and let me go in first. Who am I?

____

MAP GAME

"And having this confidence, I know that I shall abide and continue with you all for your furtherance and joy of faith." Philippians 1:25

Jesus loved others very much and had deep compassion for anyone who was suffering. Frequently He turned their suffering into joy as He cured their illnesses or even brought loved ones back to life. In this game see if you can locate the places where these miracles took place and tell what happened there.

You may wish to read about some of the miracles before you start to play the game. You can find the stories in your Bible. Here are the references:

	MIRACLE	REFERENCE	PLACE
1.	The centurion's son	Matthew 8:5-13	Capernaum
2.	The widow's son	Luke 7:11-15	Nain
3.	The deaf-mute man	Mark 7:31-37	Sidon
4.	The Greek woman's daughter	Mark 7:24-30	Tyre
5.	Raising of Lazarus	John 11:1-44	Bethany
6.	Water into wine	John 2:1-10	Cana
7.	Peter's mother-in-law	Matthew 8:14,15	Capernaum
8.	The nobleman's son	John 4:46-53	Capernaum
9.	Man with dropsy	Luke 14:1-4	Jerusalem
10.	Ten lepers	Luke 17:11-14	Between Samaria and Galilee
11.	Calmed the storm	Luke 8:22-25	Sea of Galilee
12.	Expulsion of devils	Matthew 8:28-33	Plain of Gergesenes
13.	Jairus' daughter	Mark 5:21-24, 35-43	West side of Sea of Galilee

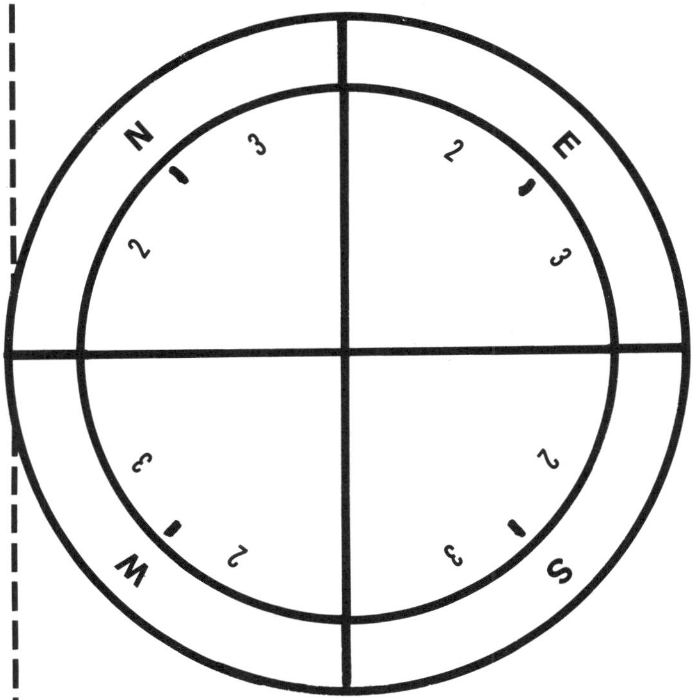

HOW TO PLAY THE GAME

1. Mount the gameboard found on the next page on heavy paper or tag, and laminate or cover with clear Con-Tact.
2. Mount the compass on heavy paper. Add a spinner. You may improvise a spinner by straightening one end of a paper clip and attaching it to the center of the compass with a brad.
3. The first player spins and moves his marker in the direction and for the number of squares indicated.
4. When the player lands on a place, he identifies the miracle which happened there. If more than one miracle happened there, any one identified will count.
5. The first player to reach and identify three places wins.

MAP GAME

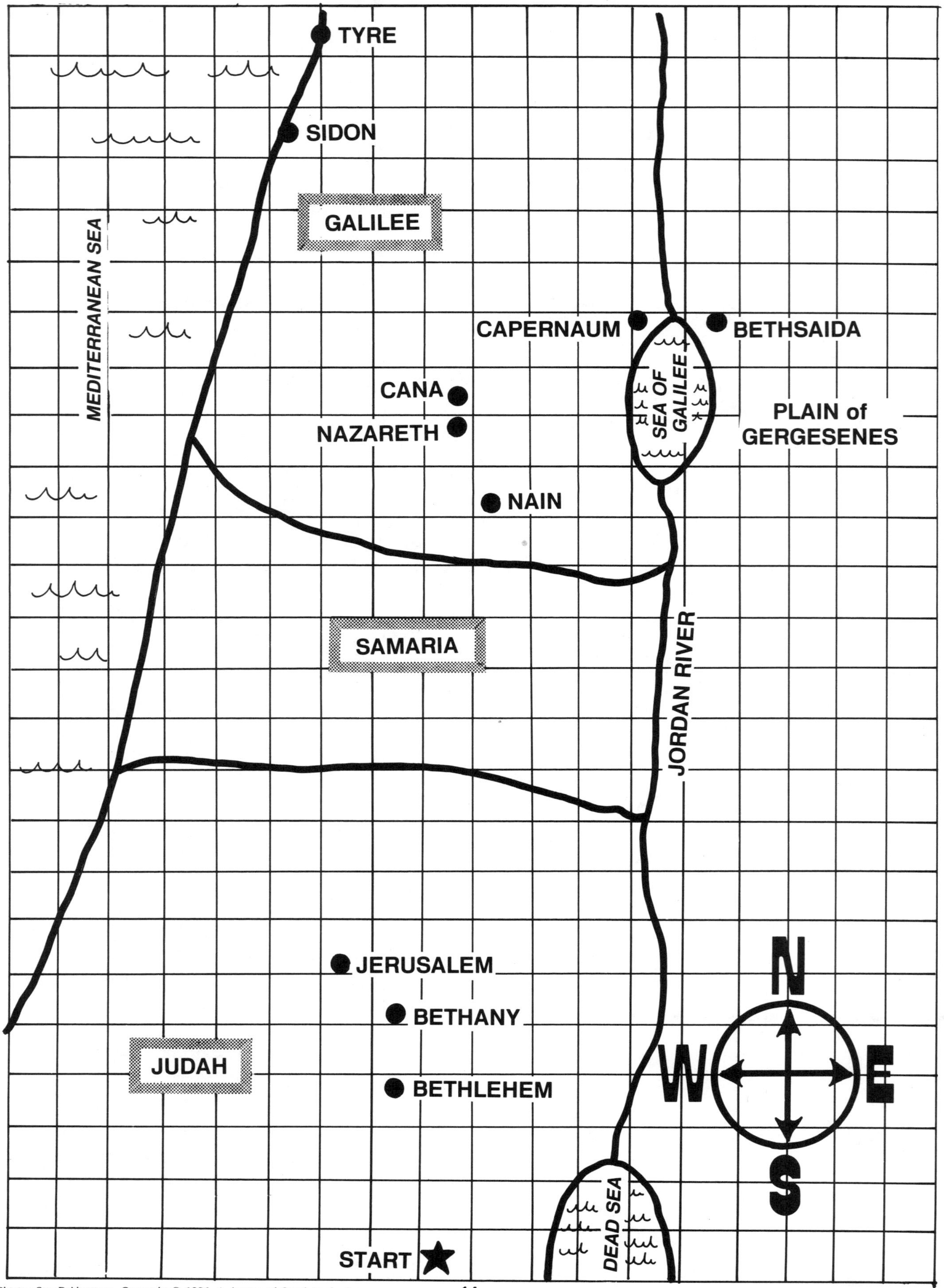

TYRE
SIDON
GALILEE
MEDITERRANEAN SEA
CAPERNAUM
BETHSAIDA
SEA OF GALILEE
CANA
NAZARETH
PLAIN of GERGESENES
NAIN
SAMARIA
JORDAN RIVER
JERUSALEM
BETHANY
JUDAH
BETHLEHEM
N
W
E
S
DEAD SEA
START

CELEBRATING JOY

PARTY INVITATIONS

"For the same cause also do ye joy, and rejoice with me." Philippians 2:18

Find out what the Bible characters in the Scriptures below had to celebrate. Read the Scripture references and then write a party invitation to their guests.

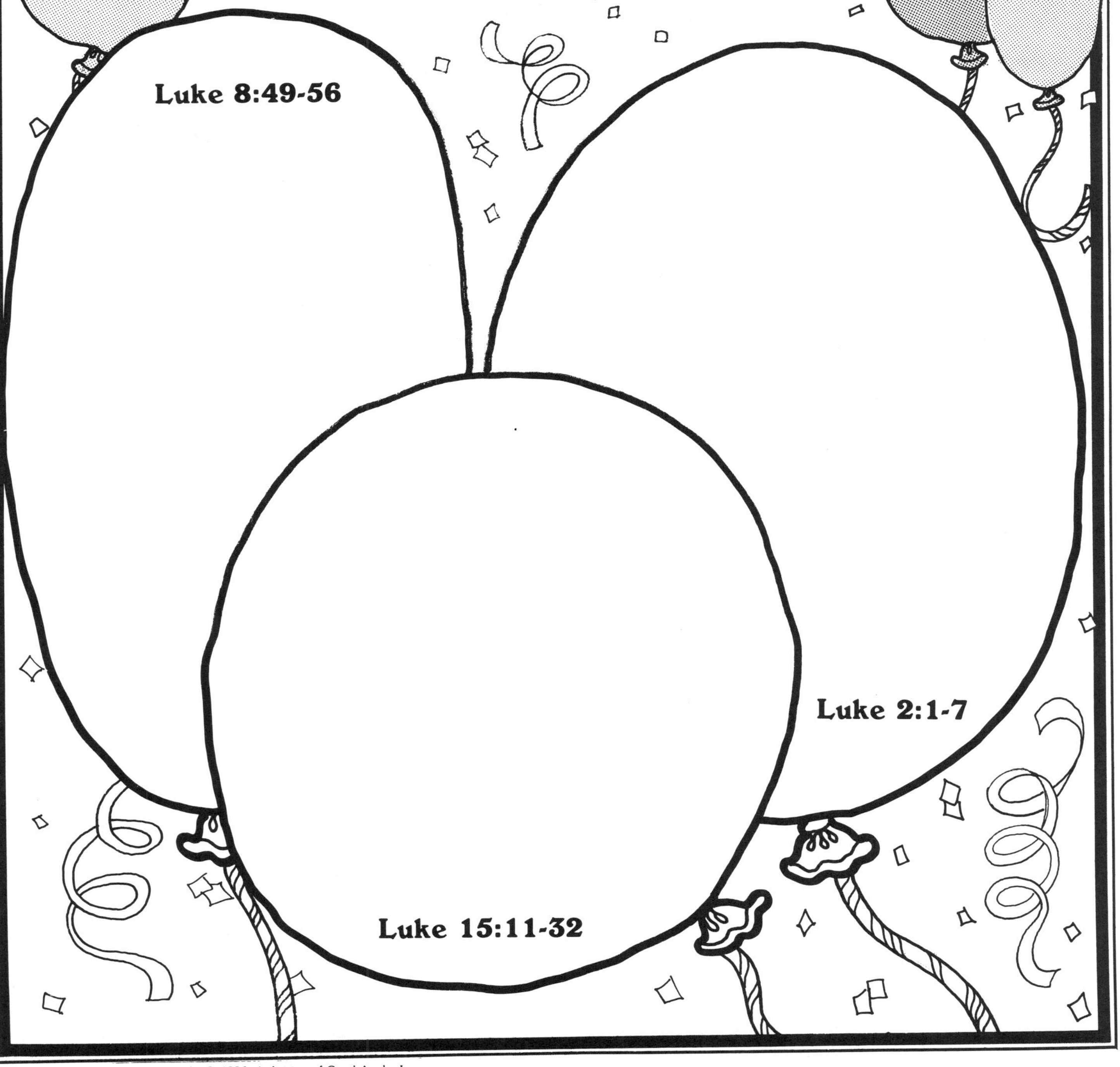

CREATE A CARTOON

There is a story in the Bible about a woman who rejoiced. Read the story first and then complete this cartoon. Continue the story in your own words and then illustrate it!

THE WOMAN WHO REJOICED

Luke 15:8,9

JUMP ROPE JINGLE

"And the angel said unto them, Fear not: for, behold, I bring you good tidings of great joy . . . ."
Luke 2:10

Read Luke 2:1-20 and write a jump rope jingle about Jesus' birth in Bethlehem.

BIBLICAL TELEGRAMS

"And these things write we unto you, that your joy may be full." I John 1:4

On each telegram on the right, write a message from one biblical character to another. Limit each message to ten words or less. Try to convey a strong feeling about joys that have been experienced. Be sure to sign the telegrams. Give a Scriptural reference for each one.

The following passages would be appropriate to use:

Matthew	13:44
Matthew	28:1-8
Matthew	2:1-10
Luke	15:11-32
Luke	15:4-7

MID-EASTERN UNION

To: ____________________

Message:

Scripture reference:

MID-EASTERN UNION

To: ____________________

Message:

Scripture reference:

MID-EASTERN UNION

To: ____________________

Message:

Scripture reference:

JOY OUT OF SORROW

"But rejoice, inasmuch as ye are partakers of Christ's sufferings; that, when his glory shall be revealed, ye may be glad also with exceeding joy." I Peter 4:13

God brings joy into our hearts in many ways. Can you identify these people to whom God brought great happiness? Read each clue at the right. Write the person's name on the blanks at the left. If you need help, look up the Scripture reference given to discover the answer. Then rearrange the circled letters to quote a message of joy.

1. (◯) ___ ___ ___ ___ ___ — She prayed many years for the joy of this day. (1 Samuel 1:12-20)

2. ___ ___ ___ ___ ___ ___ ___ (◯) ___ — She named her son John. (Luke 1:57-64)

3. (◯) ___ ___ ___ ___ ___ ___ — He was so happy he gave a great feast when his son was weaned. (Gen. 21:1-8)

4. ___ ___ ___ (◯) — The angel told her about Jesus. (Luke 1:30, 31)

5. ___ ___ ___ ___ (◯) ___ — God promised him that he would see Jesus. (Luke 2:25-33)

6. (◯) ___ ___ ___ ___ — Goliath was sorry to meet him. (1 Samuel 17:48,49)

7. ___ ___ ___ (◯) ___ ___ — His daughter came back to life. (Mark 5:22,23; 35-42)

8. ___ (◯) ___ ___   ___ ___ ___ ___ ___ — Jesus promised to take him into heaven. (Luke 23:40-43)

9. ___ ___ ___ ___ ___ (◯) ___ ___ ___ — The angel appeared to him in the temple. (Luke 1: 13, 14)

10. ___ ___ (◯) ___ — They saw a star. (Matt. 2:9-11 NIV)

11. ___ ___ (◯) (◯) ___ — Jesus appeared to him in shining garments. (Mark 9:2-7) (Hint: Answer is not Peter.)

12. ___ ___ ___ (◯) ___ ___ ___ (◯) ___ ___ — Jesus cured his blindness. (Mark 10:46-52)

13. ___ ___ ___ ___ (◯) ___ ___ (◯) ___ — Angels appeared to them. (Luke 2:8,9)

14. ___ ___ ___ ___ ___ ___ (◯) ___ ___ — Jesus went to his house for dinner. (Luke 19:1-6)

15. ___ (◯) (◯) ___ ___ ___ — The angel told her Jesus had risen. (Luke 24:1-10)

16. ___ ___ ___ ___ (◯) ___ ___ — Jesus restored his life. (John 11:1-3; 38-44)

SECRET MESSAGE:

"___   ___ ___ ___ ___ ___   ___ ___ ___ ___ ___   ___ ___ ___ ___ ___

___ ___ ___ ___ . . . ."

Proverbs 17:22

PRAYER CELEBRATION

"Hitherto have ye asked nothing in my name: ask, and ye shall receive, that your joy may be full." John 16:24

HYMN: "Joy, Oh What Joy," p. 22

OPENING PRAYER: Father in heaven, we thank you for sending us Jesus. His birth brought joy to the shepherds; His teaching and miracles filled the people with joy; His resurrection gave joy to His disciples. He is truly the source of all our joy. If our hearts are open to Jesus and His love, we will also be filled with joy. Amen.

FIRST READING: John 16:22-24 (An adaptation)
One day I will see you again and your heart will rejoice. This joy no one will be able to take from you. Before this you have never asked the Father for anything in my name. Now I say this to you. Mention the name Jesus when you are praying. Then whatever you ask for, you will receive. Your joy will be full!

SILENT PRAYER: (Children silently pray to Jesus in their hearts.)

JOY BOMBARDMENT:

Leader: Now let us thank Jesus for all the joys we have already received.
Thank you, Jesus, for the joy my friend gives me . . .
Thank you, Jesus, for celebrations that give me joy . . .
(Children spontaneously add their own.)

SECOND READING: Psalm 100 (An adaptation)
Rejoice in the Lord always;
The Lord is our God. He made us. We are His children.
Rejoice in the Lord always;
Go into His church with praise.
Give thanks to Him and bless His name.
Rejoice in the Lord always;
Our Lord is good. He is kind and loving.
He has been good to our fathers as well as to us.
Rejoice in the Lord always.

Leader: Now let us follow the example of Jesus and share our joy with others. (Each child takes a slip of paper from the "Joy Jar," p. 28. On the paper is written a suggestion of how to bring joy to someone else.)

BLESSING: May the Lord Jesus continue to fill our hearts to the brim with joy. May we go forth sharing this joy with those we meet!

JOY IN MY HEART

Words by
Helen Kitchell Evans

Music by
Frances Mann Benson

JOY, OH WHAT JOY

Words by
Helen Kitchell Evans

Music by
Frances Mann Benson

A FIVE-SENSE POEM

"For we have great joy . . . ." Philemon 1:7

JOY is the color of a rainbow.
It sounds like children laughing.
It tastes like peppermint candy
And smells like oven-baked cookies.
JOY looks like dancing firecrackers.
It makes you feel wonderful!

Write a "five-sense" poem on **JOY.** Follow this formula:

Line 1: Tell what color joy is.
Line 2: Tell what joy sounds like.
Line 3: Tell what it tastes like.
Line 4: Tell what it smells like.
Line 5: Tell what joy looks like.
Line 6: Tell how it makes you feel.

Illustrate your poem and share it with a friend.

CROSSWORD PUZZLE

"... they may do it with joy ...." Hebrews 13:17

ACROSS

3. We bring them joy.
4. Glad
8. Joy here forever
13. On happy faces
14. Jump with joy
18. We want to_______good.
19. Showed praise with applause
21. Felt joy
22. As warm_______a kitten
23. The shape of a valentine
25. A joyful sound
26. Supreme Being
27. Break God's law
31. What you do with a worm and a pole
34. Great pleasure
35. To emit rays of light
37. Tells of a sale
38. The playthings we share with others

DOWN

1. Gladness
2. One who wants to be joyful
5. Desserts
6. Container
7. Save
9. Someone important (abbr.)
10. Girl's dress
11. Give joy
12. Heaven_______our greatest joy.
14. If something hurts, it is _______________.
15. Place of rest
16. Most desirable
17. Carol (verb)
18. Happiness
20. Heaven
24. Attempt
25. Care deeply
26. Present
28. Word of a song
29. Power
30. Feeling pleased
32. Over an angel's head
33. Request
36. An abbreviation for our country

Cut out this slot.

Cut out this slot.

BIBLE SLIDE RULE

This slide rule can be made by the children and used in many ways. It is a good way to have Bible verses at your fingertips. It can also serve as a self-testing method for memory work. The child covers the verse window and reads the Scripture reference. After reciting the verse, the child can check his or her work by viewing the top window. The children will find many other ways to use this Bible aid.

DIRECTIONS:

1. Duplicate the slide rule and card so that each child will have his or her own copy.
2. Cut out the slide rule and card along the dotted lines.
3. Glue the card and slide rule onto light cardboard. Reinforce by covering with clear Con-Tact paper or laminating.
4. Cut out the two slots on the cover side of the slide rule.
5. Fold down the center line.
6. Fold up the flap and paste or glue to the back cover.
7. Place the card in the slide rule and adjust with the first verse showing in the top window. The appropriate Scripture reference will appear in the bottom window.

JOY

". . . my spirit hath rejoiced in God my Saviour."

"Now the God of hope fill you with all joy . . . ."

". . . ask, and ye shall receive, that your joy may be full."

"I have no greater joy than to hear that my children walk in truth."

". . . abide in my love . . . that your joy might be full."

Luke 1:47

Romans 15:13

John 16:24

3 John 1:4

John 15:10, 11

JOY CALENDAR

"Rejoice ye in that day, and leap for joy . . . ." Luke 6:23

	1 Matthew 2:10	2 Luke 1:14	3 John 15:11	4 Acts 8:8	
5 Romans 15:32	6 2 Corinthians 2:3	7 Philippians 2:2	8 I Thessalonians 2:20	9 2 Timothy 1:4	10 Philemon 1:7
11 Hebrews 13:17	12 James 4:9	13 I Peter 4:13	14 I John 1:4	15 Jude 24	16 Matthew 13:44
17 Luke 2:10	18 John 16:22	19 Acts 15:3	20 Romans 14:17	21 2 Corinthians 1:24	22 Philippians 1:25
23 I Thessalonians 2:19	24 Philemon 1:20	25 Hebrews 12:2	26 James 1:2	27 I Peter 1:8	28 2 John 12
29 3 John 4	30 Matthew 25:23	31 Luke 8:13			

Each day this month, read the corresponding Scripture about joy. When you have read the verse, draw a happy face in the box.

★This award can be made from ribbons or construction paper. Present it to the student who smiles and shares the most joy during the week.

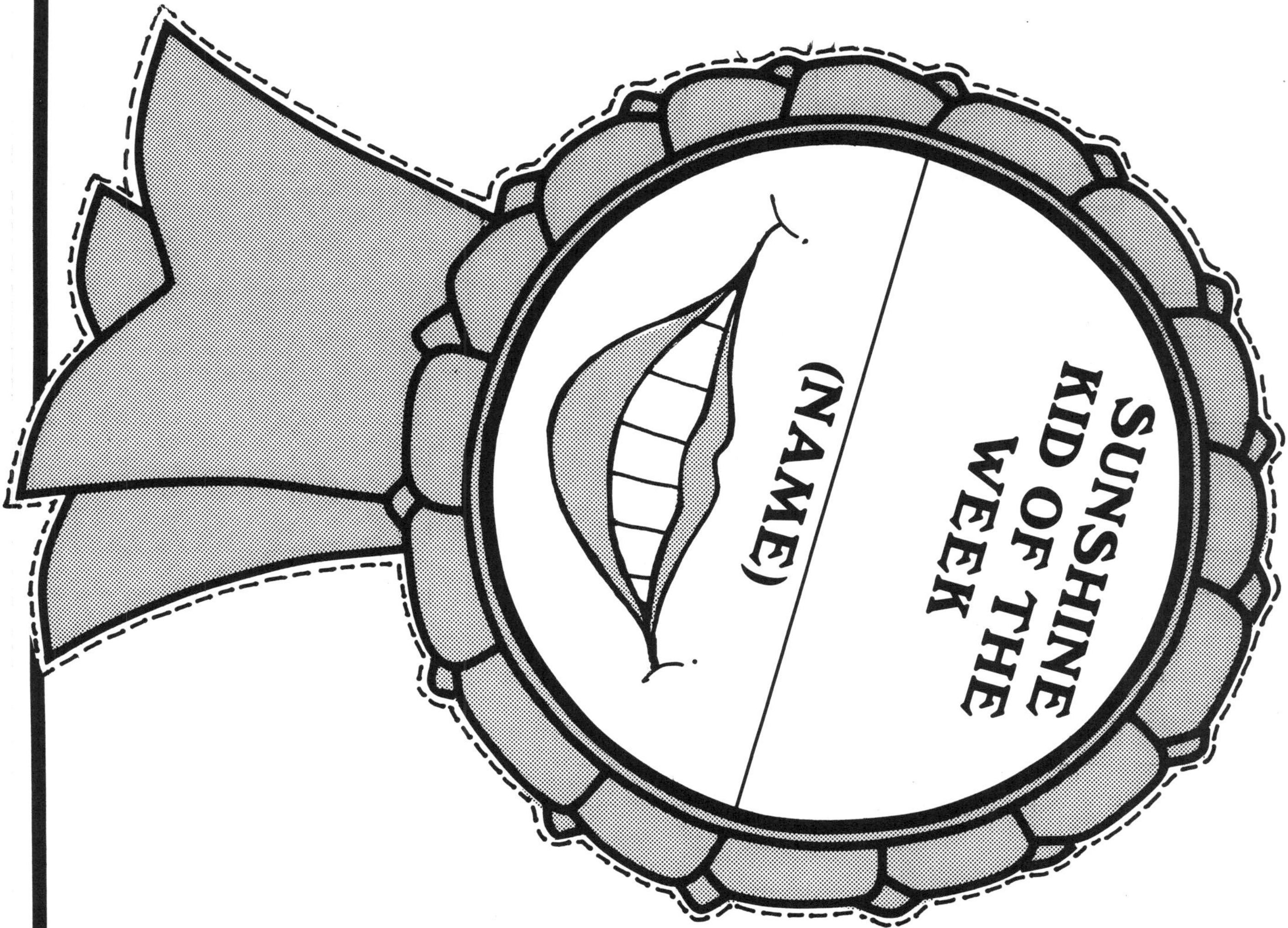

★This note can be sent by anyone wishing to share a joy.

I'M JUMPING FOR JOY BECAUSE

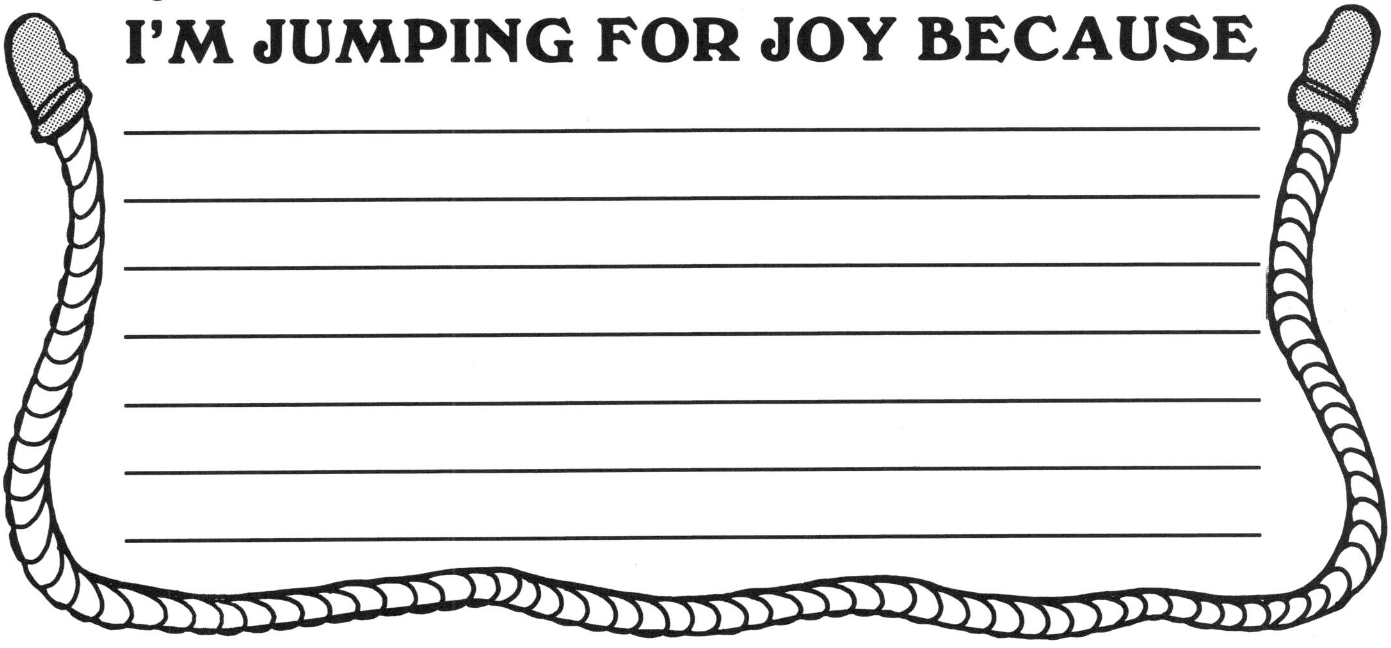

SHARING JOY

SHARE YOUR JOYS

"For ye are our glory and joy." I Thessalonians 2:20

JOY JAR

Keep a jar in your classroom with slips of paper and a pencil nearby. Whenever anyone has a joy to share, it can be written down and put in the jar. At the end of the week, the jar will be filled to the brim with joys! Read each joy aloud to the students for all to share.

Try the following variation: On slips of paper, write different ways to bring joy to others. Students can come and pick one from the jar and try to make another person happy.

JOKE FILE

Make a joke file for your classroom. Collect funny jokes and put them in the file. Have plain index cards available so the students can add to the joke file. A joke can be shared with another when this person is sad; a joke can be slipped inside a get-well card, etc.

JOY WALK

Take the children for a walk in the park. Have them listen to all the joyful noises around them—birds chirping, bees buzzing, children laughing, etc. Sit under a tree and discuss all the sounds they hear. Enjoy a snack together!

NOVELTY LETTERS

Have the children write novelty letters to someone in the Bible.

SIGN LANGUAGE

Teach the children the sign language for joy!

JOY STICKERS

"These things have I spoken unto you, that my joy might remain in you, and that your joy might be full." John 15:11

Design your own stickers using Scripture verses about JOY. Cut them out and give them to your friends. A little glue on the back will help them stick to book covers, book bags, lunch bags and school folders!

SUGGESTED SCRIPTURE VERSES:

"But the fruit of the Spirit is . . . joy . . . ." (Galatians 5:22)

"I have no greater joy than to hear that my children walk in truth." (3 John 4)

" . . . rejoice with joy . . . ." (I Peter 1:8)

" . . . the kingdom of God is . . . joy . . . ." (Romans 14:17)

" . . . your heart shall rejoice . . . ." (John 16:22)

FORTUNE COOKIE SURPRISE

''And thou shalt have joy and gladness . . . .'' Luke 1:14

Suggested Scriptural passages about joy are found on page 48. Write your favorites on the slips of paper provided below. Insert the slips of paper inside fortune cookies. Invite your friends over for a party. Take turns reading the verses you received before eating your treats!

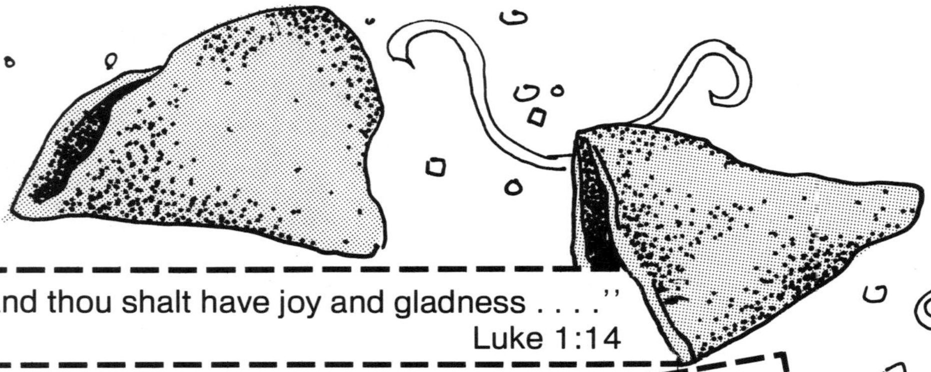

''And thou shalt have joy and gladness . . . .''
Luke 1:14

THE IDEAL CITY

"And there was great joy in that city." Acts 8:8

Imagine you are building an ideal city. List five buildings that you would include and explain why you have chosen them.

1.
2.
3.
4.
5.

List five people whom you would like to bring to this ideal city. They could be members of your family, friends, biblical figures, historical personalities, or contemporary people. Explain why you value the ones you have chosen.

1.
2.
3.
4.
5.

You will be given the basic necessities to live (food, clothing, shelter, etc.). Now list five specific items you would want to make sure you had available in this ideal city.

1.
2.
3.
4.
5.

List five dreams or goals that you would have for this ideal city.

1.
2.
3.
4.
5.

List five gifts that you would like to give to the people in this ideal city.

1.
2.
3.
4.
5.

If you were funded a million dollars per year to be used to remedy five evils or enhance five causes, what five would you choose?

1.
2.
3.
4.
5.

JOYFUL NEWS

"Having many things to write unto you . . . that our joy may be full." II John 12

Use the pattern below to make a mailer, or duplicate the page. Cut out the mailer. On the opposite side, write a special letter to a friend, sharing a joy that is in your heart. Decorate it with happy designs, address it and mail!

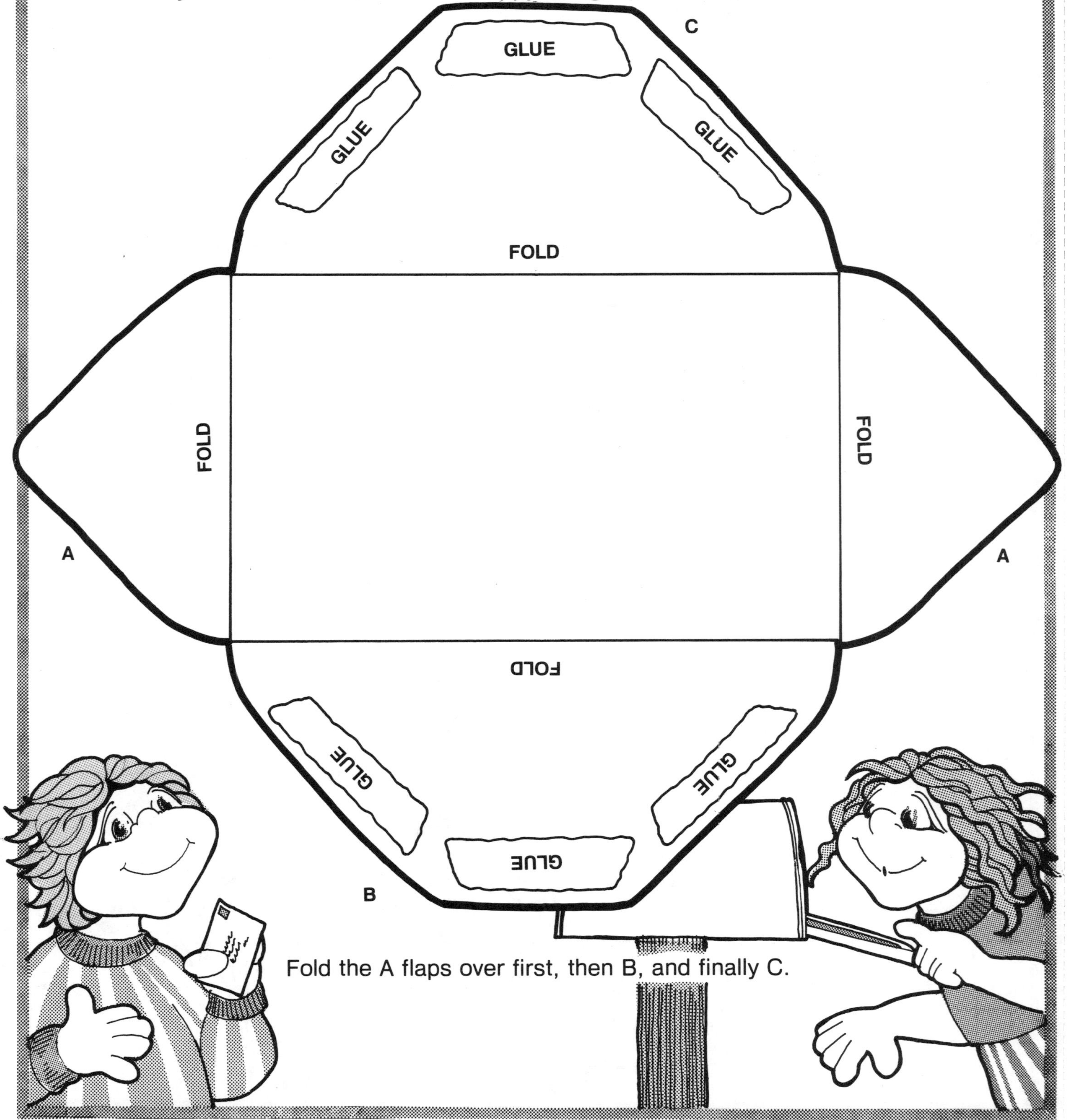

Fold the A flaps over first, then B, and finally C.

SMILES

"Now the God of hope fill you with all joy . . . ." Romans 15:13

These are some things that make me SMILE!

My dad SMILES when

My friend SMILES when

My mom SMILES when

My teacher SMILES when

These are some things that I can do for others to make them SMILE!

TOP BILLING

"And now come I to thee; and these things I speak in the world, that they might have my joy fulfilled in themselves."
John 17:13

J. Billingsworth Goodman, a billionaire, wants you, an outdoor advertiser who designs and erects billboards, to help advertise his scheme to bring joy to some troubled spot in today's world. He will contribute the money, but he also wants to alert others by encouraging them to contribute something according to their special talents.

Pick the troubled spot and design the billboard in the space below. Define and highlight the problem; then suggest some solution. You may use words and/or pictures in your design.

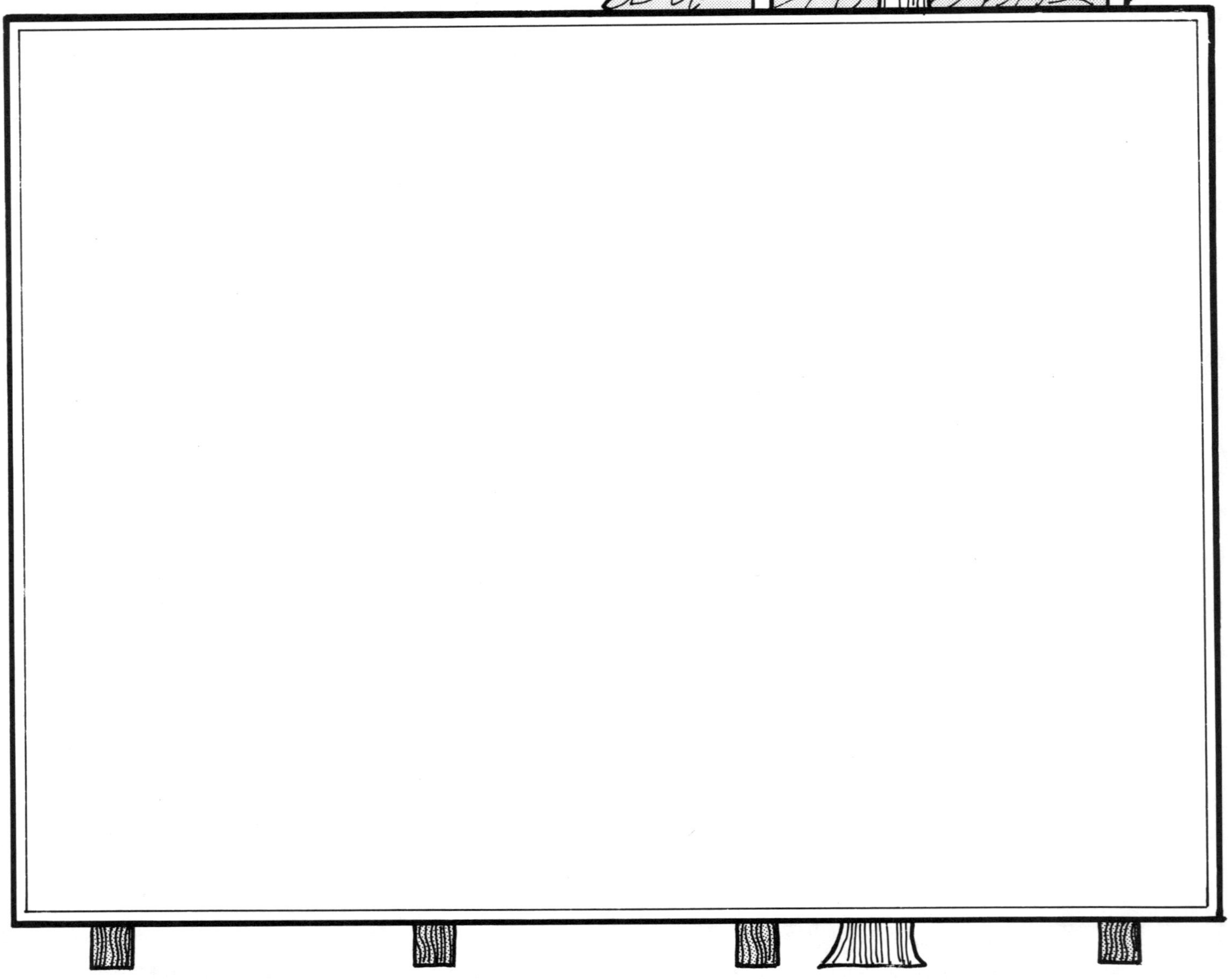

CLOUD CHASERS

"Be afflicted, and mourn, and weep: let your laughter be turned to mourning, and your joy to heaviness." James 4:9

Make rainbows in someone's life by doing something which will bring him joy. Then write two or three words to describe your action in one of the spaces below and color the rainbow. See how long it will take to complete all the rainbows. Hang this sheet in your room. You may have brought so much joy that your life will have rainbows also, and you will want to start another sheet to match this.

STAR BRIGHT

"When they saw the star, they rejoiced with exceeding great joy." Matthew 2:10

DIRECTIONS:

1. Using a paper plate or bowl, make a basket.
2. Cut the plate/bowl in half.
3. Sew around the edges with yarn.
4. Stitch the two sides together to fasten, or staple.
5. Decorate the outside of your basket.
6. Make a handle for your basket with pipe cleaners.
7. Fill the basket with stars for your family and friends.

STARS:

1. Use the star pattern on the right.
2. Write the name of one of your family or friends on the star.
3. On the other side, write a message that will give him joy.
4. Decorate your star.

Here are some messages you might like to use:

1. You are my rainbow.
2. You help me sail to my dreams.
3. Thanks for always being there to pull me through.
4. God's in charge.
5. The Lord protect you.
6. For someone who knows all about me and still loves me.
7. His presence go with you.
8. I hold you in my heart.
9. You are loved by God and by me.
10. You rise above the ordinary.
11. God bless you.
12. God makes you special.

Give your stars to your family or friends for a special day.

FLOWERING JOY

"But he that received the seed into stony places, the same is he that heareth the word, and anon with joy receiveth it." Matthew 13:20

Make someone happy and give her a flower! If the following ideas give joy to those around you, draw flowers on the plants. If the ideas do not bring happiness, finish the bouquets as weeds. Then color the plants and flowers as a sign of the growth in your own life.

Take care of things which belong to others.

Keep promises you make.

Be patient with others.

Always tell the truth.

Get even with someone who hurt you.

Experiment with alcohol.

Laugh at faults of others.

Help your father cut the grass.

Obey your parents.

Clean your room.

Do your homework well.

Cheat on a test.

Pray every morning and evening.

Talk about your classmates.

SHOUT FOR JOY!

OBJECTIVE: This bulletin board encourages children to share their joys with others.

VARIATIONS: 1. Other appropriate titles would be:

Rejoice in the Lord!
Sing out with Joy to the Lord!
To Have Joy One Must Share It!
Happiness Was Born a Twin!
(Old Indian Saying)

2. Children can attach notes to the bulletin board sharing joys they have experienced during the week.

Examples: My mom had a baby girl!
My grandma is out of the hospital!

RECEIVING JOY

FAMILY JOY

"That I may come unto you with joy by the will of God, and may with you be refreshed."
Romans 15:32

Many times we experience joy in celebrating with our families. Design four napkin rings to be used for a special dinner, picnic or party. Write the name of each family member on the napkin ring and illustrate it with happy designs and colors!

GLUE | GLUE

GLUE | GLUE

GLUE | GLUE

GLUE | GLUE

GLUE | GLUE

JOY OF NEIGHBORS

". . . ye rejoice with joy unspeakable and full of glory." I Peter 1:8

The joy which we share with the people who live in our neighborhood is an extension of the joy we share with our families. As we share happiness and joy, all of us grow. From Deuteronomy 14:29 or Deuteronomy 16:11,14, copy in the space below a part which you think is meaningful for you. In the other space, tell what you might do to have a celebration in your neighborhood. Is there anyone who should be invited who might otherwise be ignored?

For each of the letters below, give a word or phrase that describes, explains, or shows how you and your neighbors can show what it means to live and celebrate in a Christian community.

N ______________________________

E ______________________________

I ______________________________

G ______________________________

H ______________________________

B ______________________________

O ______________________________

R ______________________________

S ______________________________

BEAUTIFUL WORLD

Our hearts well up with joy when we see the beauty of the world God has created for us. In the midst of all his troubles, Job was reminded of God's care for us and His wisdom in creating this beauty.

Read the magnificent passage in chapters 38 and 39 of the book of Job where God tells us that He garmented the earth with shrubs and flowers and furnished it with animals.

Make a booklet of the environment in which we find such delight. Copy a quotation from the book of Job on the bottom of each page and make a picture to illustrate it. One person may wish to make the entire booklet, or a group may want to make one which can subsequently be placed in your school or church library.

Here is a list of some of the things you may wish to look for and put in your booklet.

- Morning stars
- Sea
- Cloud
- Darkness
- Morning
- Daylight
- Snow
- Hail
- East wind
- Lightning
- Thunder
- Rain
- Wilderness
- Dew
- Buds
- Ice
- Hoar frost
- Ravens
- Wild goats
- Lions
- Horses
- Mountains
- Eagles

Who has caused the rain to satisfy the desolate ground and caused it to bud? Job 38:26, 27

TALLY

"My brethren, count it all joy . . . ." James 1:2

God gives us joy in many different ways. Below are words which explain or show this gift of joy in life. While you are playing this game, think of how you may increase this joy in your life and in the lives of others.

MATERIALS: Gameboard; word cards; and set of very small cards each having one letter printed on it (5 to 10 cards for each letter) placed face up on the table; tally cards.

DIRECTIONS: Mount the gameboard and words on heavy paper or tag, and laminate or cover with clear plastic. Place the words in a small box or bag, and shake to mix. Draw out one word and define, explain or give an example to show how God gives joy in our lives or how we give joy to others. If the answer is correct, choose a letter and place it on the grid. When the letters make a word, record the number on the grid under each letter. Letters are left on the grid and may be used again if they spell a new word. You may take two letters for any word with a balloon. At the end of the period, total your scores. The player with the highest total wins.

beatitude	paradise	obedience	bliss	rejoice
considerate	sing	concerned	blessed	smile
celebration	Christmas	kindness	Easter	unselfish
angels	Commandments	enjoyment	rules	flowers
glad	hope	peace	Holy Spirit	Jesus
laws	gift	understanding	helpful	sharing
God	heart	heaven	happiness	delight
joyous	love	laughter	pleasing	school
caring	courtesy	forgiving	generous	tolerant
giving	others	parents	playmate	trust

TALLY

1	2	3	1	2	3	1
2	3	1	2	3	1	2
3	1	2	3	1	2	3
1	2	4	1	4	3	1
2	3	1	5	3	1	2
3	1	4	3	4	2	3
1	2	3	1	2	3	1
2	3	1	2	3	1	2
3	1	2	3	1	2	3

PSALM OF JOY

Psalm 107 is a beautiful song of joy in which the singer tells of the many difficulties which the people faced and their rejoicing when God helped them.

Read the Psalm quotations described in the spaces. Then write of a situation in your life of which each reminds you. Tell how your problem was solved with God's help to your relief and your happiness and joy.

You may wish to use the back of this paper or a separate sheet for your writing.

Travellers lost in the desert verses 4-7

Shipwrecked sailors rescued from the sea verses 23-29

Hunger and thirst satisfied verses 35-37

Sick people restored to health verses 18-20

MY SONG OF JOY

"And my spirit hath rejoiced in God my Saviour." Luke 1:47

When Mary visited Elisabeth, she sang a hymn of joy to the Lord. Read Luke 1:46-55. Then write your own joyful prayer to the Lord. On the lines provided, write about all the wonderful things the Lord has done for you. Illustrate your prayer.

My soul magnifies the Lord,

And my spirit finds joy in God my Savior.

For He that is mighty has done great things for me.

He has ______________________________.

He has ______________________________.

He has ______________________________.

He has ______________________________.

And He has ______________________________.

JOY FLAG

"... that I may be filled with joy." II Timothy 1:4

Create your own joy flag from tagboard or poster paper. A dowel rod can serve as the staff. Print your name in large letters on the flag. Design the rim with objects and words that give you joy. Hang your flag in your room or tack it to your bulletin board!

ANSWER KEY

HAPPINESS ROAD p. 5
Suggested Answers

Talk to God often in your heart.—" . . . pray to thy Father which is in secret . . . ." Matthew 6:6
Tell the truth.—"Thou shalt not bear false witness . . . ." Exodus 20:16
Don't be jealous of a friend's new dress.—"Thou shalt not covet . . . ." Exodus 20:17
Remember that marriage is holy.—"Thou shalt not commit adultery." Exodus 20:14
Don't steal candy from store.—"Thou shalt not steal." Exodus 20:15
Be a good sport and a good loser.—"And as ye would that men should do to you, do ye also to them likewise." Luke 6:31
Attend church.—"Remember the sabbath day, to keep it holy." Exodus 20:8
Forgive someone who hurts you.—" . . . forgive us our debts, as we forgive our debtors . . . ." Matthew 6:12
Do what your parents tell you.—"Honour thy father and thy mother . . . ." Exodus 20:12
Do not use God's name when angry.—"Thou shalt not take the name of the Lord thy God in vain . . . ." Exodus 20:7
Do not hit or hurt people—Luke 6:31
Be satisfied with what you have.—Exodus 20:17
Do not cheat on homework.—Exodus 20:15
Offer to do dishes for your mother.—Luke 6:31

ROAD BLOCKS p. 8

PROBLEM	REFERENCE	PARABLE
Pride	Luke 18:9-14	Pharisee and the tax collector
Greed	Mark 10:20-22	The rich young man
Anger	Matthew 5:21	Anger and reconciliation
Envy	Luke 15:25-32	Prodigal son
Laziness	Matthew 25:1-13	The ten maidens
Fear	Luke 12:4-7	Warnings and encouragements
Unwillingness to forgive	Matthew 18:21,22	Forgiveness
Ambition	Luke 14:7-11	Marriage feast
Hatred	Matthew 5:43-48	Love for enemies

JOY TRAIL p. 10

". . . let all those that put their trust in thee rejoice: let them ever shout for joy. . . ."

RIDDLES p. 11

1. Women
2. Mary Magdalene
3. Jesus
4. Stone
5. Angel
6. Soldiers

MORE RIDDLES p. 12

7. Disciples
8. John
9. High priests
10. Thomas
11. Cloths
12. Peter

JOY OUT OF SORROW p. 19

1. Hannah
2. Elisabeth
3. Abraham
4. Mary
5. Simeon
6. David
7. Jairus
8. Good Thief
9. Zacharias
10. Magi
11. James
12. Bartimaeus
13. Shepherds
14. Zacchaeus
15. Joanna
16. Lazarus

SECRET MESSAGE:
"A merry heart doeth good . . . ." Proverbs 17:22

CROSSWORD PUZZLE p. 24

ACROSS	DOWN
3. Others	1. Joy
4. Happy	2. Me
8. Heaven	5. Pies
13. Smiles	6. Pan
14. Skip	7. Keep
18. Be	9. VIP
19. Clapped	10. Smock
21. Rejoiced	11. Please
22. As	12. Is
23. Heart	14. Sore
25. Laughter	15. Bed
26. God	16. Best
27. Violate	17. Sing
31. Fish	18. Beatitude
34. Delight	20. Paradise
35. Shine	24. Try
37. Ad	25. Love
38. Toys	26. Gift
	28. Lyric
	29. Might
	30. Glad
	32. Halo
	33. Ask
	36. U.S.

SCRIPTURAL PASSAGES ON JOY

Matthew 2:10; 13:20; 13:44; 25:21; 25:23; 28:8
Luke 1:14; 1:44; 2:10; 6:23; 8:13; 10:17; 15:7; 15:10; 24:41; 24:52
John 16:20; 16:21; 16:22; 16:24; 17:13
Acts 2:28; 8:8; 13:52; 15:3; 20:24
Romans 5:11; 14:17; 15:13; 15:32
2 Corinthians 1:24; 2:3; 7:13; 8:2
Galatians 5:22
Philippians 1:4; 1:25; 2:2; 2:17; 2:18; 4:1
I Thessalonians 1:6; 2:19; 2:20; 3:9
2 Timothy 1:4
Philemon 1:7; 1:20
Hebrews 12:2; 13:17
James 1:2; 4:9
I Peter 1:8; 4:13